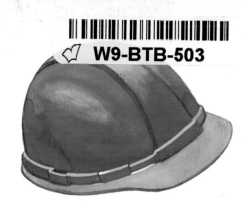

# THE HOME DEPOT®

# BIG BOOK OF TOOLS

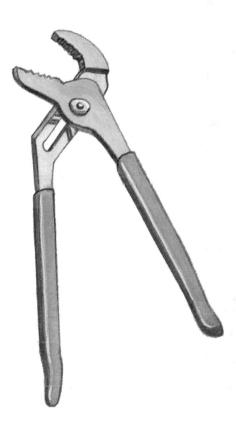

by **Kimberly Weinberger**
**Illustrated by Tom LaPadula**

SCHOLASTIC INC.

Cartwheel BOOKS®

New York   Toronto   London   Auckland   Sydney   Mexico City   New Delhi   Hong Kong

# HOME IMPROVEMENT

**F**rom the basement to the roof, a home could not be built without tools. Once a home is completed, having the right tools on hand will keep it running smoothly and looking its best. This book will introduce you to the many tools people use in their homes. Remember, any project that needs a tool also needs a grown-up. And don't forget the most important rule of home improvement: safety first!

## GROWN-UP TOOL RULE

While tools can be a big help when fixing and building, they can also be very dangerous if used the wrong way. Always ask a grown-up to show you how a tool works. And never use any tool — even if you know how it works — without having a grown-up help you.

## WORK GLOVES

Work gloves can be made of rubber, heavy canvas, or leather, and they can keep harmful or messy liquids from touching your skin. Some gloves are specially made to protect you from burns or fire. The gloves you choose will depend on each particular project.

## DUST MASK

Fine dust and tiny droplets of glue or paint can be dangerous to breathe. A paper dust mask that fits over your mouth and nose will help you breathe easily and safely. Toxic materials should only be used in a properly ventilated area.

## TOOL BELT

Tool belts worn around the waist provide easy, hands-free access to the tools you need. Some tool belts can also support your hardworking back muscles.

## SAFETY GOGGLES

Safety goggles protect your eyes from dust and flying bits of material. Always use eye protection when working with tools.

## HEARING PROTECTORS

Tools can be noisy! To block out loud sounds, always wear padded earmuffs to protect your hearing.

**TOOL TIP**

Broken, rusty, or missing tools aren't much help when you're faced with a home improvement project. Keep your tools in a clean, dry, organized place so they'll always be ready to help you tackle any job.

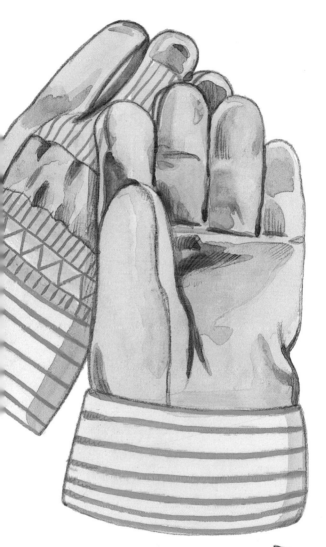

## HARD HAT

Wearing a padded hard hat made from shock-resistant materials will help to keep your head protected.

## KNEEPADS

Working on floors or under sinks can mean spending hours on your knees. Kneepads provide a foam cushion to support your knees in comfort. Most have a slip-resistant surface to keep you from sliding.

# PLUMBING

**D**rip. Drip. Drip. The faucet on this kitchen sink is leaking. Before you begin, be sure to turn off the water supply. To fix the problem, the faucet handle must be removed. Use a screwdriver to remove the handle's cap. A pair of pliers unscrews the brass stem assembly beneath. A utility knife cuts off a worn-out, rubber O-ring from the stem. A new O-ring is needed to make a tight seal. Presto! The leak is fixed.

# PLUMBING

## SCREWDRIVERS

Screwdrivers come in many different sizes so that they can be used with different size screws. Some are very long for reaching into tight spaces. Others are small enough to fit in your pocket. Some screwdrivers have rubber handles for added comfort.

### RATCHET NUT DRIVER

For a hex-shaped nut or bolt, a ratchet nut driver is the right choice.

### PHILLIPS® SCREWDRIVER

A Phillips® screwdriver is needed for a screw that has a small X on its head.

### SLOTTED SCREWDRIVER

A slotted screwdriver is needed when a screw has a single slot across its head.

### UTILITY KNIFE

A utility knife is the best tool for cutting through soft materials. The blade is very sharp! When not in use, the blade should be lowered inside its protective case by sliding down the lever on the handle.

### TOILET PLUNGER

A toilet plunger has a large, rubber suction cup attached to a long wooden handle. When a pipe is clogged, the water cannot drain properly. To fix it, the suction cup is placed over the drain and pressed up and down quickly. The rush of air helps loosen the clog so it flows easily away.

## WRENCHES

Plumbing problems often call for the help of a wrench. Wrenches are made for gripping objects such as pipes, nuts, or bolts.

### ALLEN® WRENCH

An Allen® wrench is a steel rod shaped like the letter L.

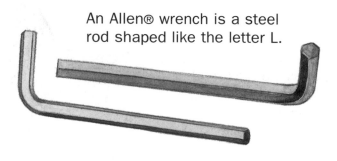

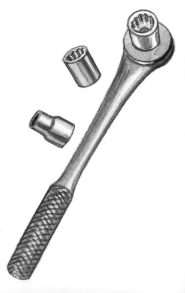

### SOCKET WRENCH

A socket wrench has a rounded hole on its end. Different sockets can be placed into the hole to turn nuts and bolts of different sizes.

## PLIERS

There are many types of pliers, each specially made for different jobs.

## NEEDLE-NOSE PLIERS

Needle-nose pliers have long, thin jaws that make them perfect for gripping and fitting into tight spaces.

## SLIP-JOINT PLIERS

Slip-joint pliers are used for gripping small objects. They have slightly curved jaws with teeth and a hinge that allows the opening to range from wide to narrow.

## LINESMAN'S PLIERS

Linesman's pliers are good for gripping small objects, as well as for cutting wire or metal.

## PIPE WRENCH

A pipe wrench is a large, heavy tool with an adjustable jaw. It helps grip and turn large bolts and pipes.

## STRAP WRENCH

A strap wrench lets you turn objects that are odd sizes. They are helpful when you need to protect the finish.

## ADJUSTABLE WRENCH

An adjustable wrench has a knob on the side of its head called a knurl screw. Turning the knurl screw makes the jaws of the wrench move closer together or farther apart.

TOOL TIP
Before putting the faucet handle back together, it's important to coat the stem assembly with waterproof grease. The grease will help the parts to last longer by making them operate more smoothly.

# PAINTING & WALLPAPERING

Can you picture the walls of your bedroom with different colors and patterns? Maybe you see walls that are sky blue, sea green, or covered with dots and stripes. It's easy to make whatever you imagine come to life with the right tools. This bedroom is getting a coat of paint on one wall and wallpaper on another. First, both walls are washed, rinsed, patched, and sanded to make them smooth. A paint roller and paintbrushes are used to apply paint to one wall. A smoothing brush, wide broadknife, razor knife, and seam roller are needed to make the wallpaper look perfect.

## PUTTY KNIFE

A putty knife is used to patch holes and cracks by applying a type of wet plaster called spackle. The flat, flexible blade helps spread the spackle evenly.

## SANDING BLOCK

A block covered with fine sandpaper smoothes the spackle once it has dried completely. Gently rubbing the sanding block around the entire area gets rid of any bumps, bubbles, or rough spots.

## PAINTBRUSHES

Paintbrushes are available in many shapes and sizes. The bristles can be angled, chisel-shaped, or straight. They are used to apply paint to any inside or outside surface. Synthetic bristles work well with oil-based and latex paints. Natural bristles work well with oil-based paints. Nylon bristles work well with water-based paints.

## PAINT ROLLER

A paint roller has a soft cover made of wool, polyester, or foam that fits over its roller bar. The rolling action of a paint roller helps spread paint evenly across large areas of a wall.

# SMOOTHING BRUSH

A smoothing brush has a wooden handle with a wide, flat bristle base. The bristles are used to smooth wrinkles or air bubbles once the paper is applied to the wall.

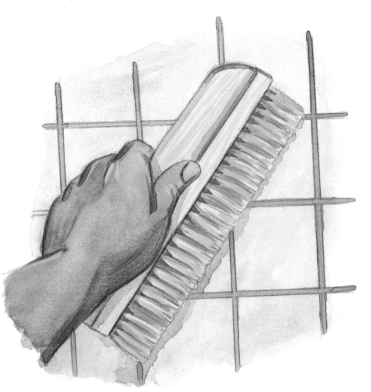

## SEAM ROLLER

When the wallpaper is in place, a seam roller is used. It presses the paper firmly to the wall and helps prevent the edges from peeling.

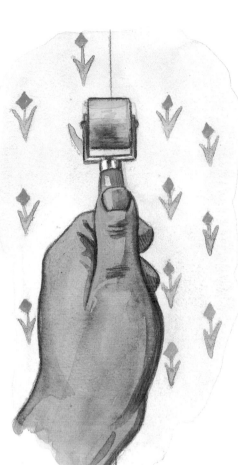

## BROADKNIFE and RAZOR KNIFE

A broadknife has a wooden handle and a very wide, flat blade. It is used to hold an edge of wallpaper in place while any extra paper is trimmed away. A sharp razor knife is run along the edge of the broadknife, cleanly cutting the excess paper.

## PLASTIC SMOOTHER

Another tool used for wallpapering is a flexible plastic smoother. It uses a plastic edge instead of bristles to iron out problem areas.

## TOOL TIP

When working with a paintbrush, try to use long, slow strokes. Dip only the top end of the bristles into the paint can. Then gently tap the brush to remove any extra paint that might drip.

## CIRCULAR SAW

A circular saw is a power tool. It has a sharp spinning blade shaped like a disk. This blade makes cutting wood easy and fast. It is also very dangerous and, like all power tools, should only be used by a grown-up.

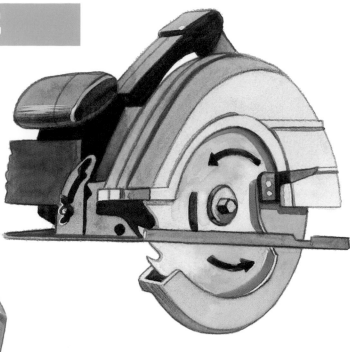

## TAPE MEASURE

A tape measure is used to measure objects and spaces. It has a plastic or metal case and a thin, steel measuring tape coiled inside. It also has a switch for locking the tape in place. Be sure to release the switch carefully— the thin, steel edges can be sharp!

## JIGSAW

A jigsaw is a power saw with a thin blade and tiny, sharp teeth. A large handgrip on top of the saw guides the blade as it cuts through wood or other materials. The jigsaw is a power tool and should only be used by a grown-up.

## PRY BAR

A pry bar is a steel tool used to pull off wood that has been nailed in place. Sometimes called a "cat's paw" because of its shape, this tool has a bent head with two claws. A small space between the claws is used for hooking the head of a nail.

## CHAINSAW

Chainsaws are used to cut tree limbs or logs. To prevent injury all power tools should only be used by an adult.

# POWER DRILL

Another power tool that should only be used by a grown-up is the power drill. It is used to drill holes in wood or other materials. It has a metal tip called a bit. The bit spins very fast as it drills holes. Different size bits can be used to make small, wide, shallow, or deep holes.

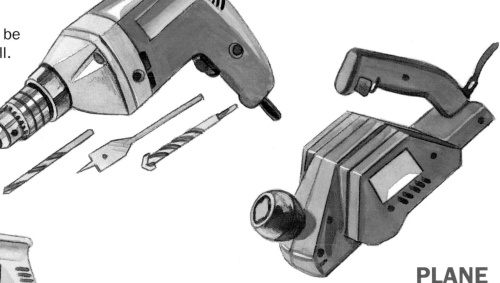

## PLANE

A plane shaves and smoothes a piece of wood with its wide, sharp blade. Planes can be handheld or powered by electricity.

## BALL-PEEN HAMMER

A ball-peen hammer has a flat, steel face for pounding nails, and a rounded, steel face for bending and shaping metal.

## HAMMER

A hammer is used for pounding nails into wood. There are many types of hammers. The most common is the nail hammer. It has a claw at one end for pulling nails and a crowned head for pounding nails.

## MALLET

A mallet has a barrel-shaped head made of hard rubber, plastic, or wood. It is used to hammer the end of another tool, such as a wood chisel.

## SLEDGE-HAMMER

A sledgehammer is a very large hammer with a rectangular head. The long handle is usually gripped with two hands in order to control the swing of this heavy tool.

## BRICKLAYER'S HAMMER

A bricklayer's hammer has a flat, steel end on one side of its head. The other side has a sharp edge that is used to cut bricks and trim stones.

**TOOL TIP**

When measuring the wall space for the shelving unit, be sure to use your tape measure at the top, middle, and bottom of the wall. Not all walls are perfectly even. By measuring three times, you'll be sure your measurements are correct.

# GARDENING

**T**urning a grassy area like this backyard into a glorious garden calls for a wide variety of tools. First, the ground must be prepared. A mason's line and powdered chalk mark the edges of the garden. A garden edger is used to cut along the chalk line. A spade cuts and removes strips of grass and soil, or sod. Fertilizer is added to help plants grow. Finally, the soil is smoothed with a garden rake. Now the garden is ready for planting!

## BRICK and CONCRETE TOOLS

### CHALK LINE and POWDERED CHALK

A chalk line, also called a mason's line, is a long, thin string usually made of cotton or nylon.

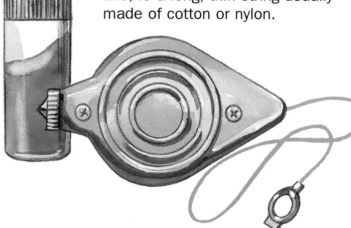

### MASON'S LINE

A mason's line is used to mark a straight line between two points. A string is coiled inside a metal container. The container is filled with powdered chalk. When the string is stretched across an area, it is plucked or snapped. This action causes a powdery chalk line to be left behind.

### GARDEN EDGER

A garden edger has a wooden handle and a blade that is shaped like the letter D. When the edger is pushed into the ground, its blade cuts through soil and roots.

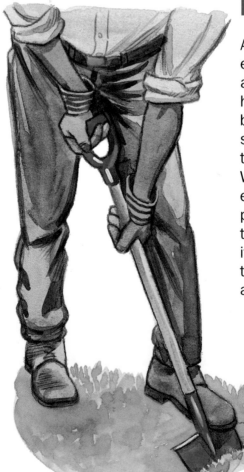

### SOD LIFTER

A sod lifter has a long handle that is slightly bent. Its thin, steel head is rounded, and it can easily cut into and remove a layer of sod.

### HOE

A garden hoe has a tapered, beveled blade attached to a long handle. The garden hoe is used for chopping and weeding.

### HAND TROWEL

A hand trowel is a small shovel. It is used for removing and depositing small amounts of soil when planting seeds.

## SPADE

A spade is a large shovel that is used for cutting into soil and digging. You can use your foot to push the flat, steel edge of the spade into the ground.

## LEVEL HEAD RAKE

A level head rake has a flat top, a long handle, and steel teeth. The flat top is good for spreading mulch, peat moss, and soil. It is also used to level beds for seed. The tines, or prongs, are used to remove debris or break up soil.

**TOOL TIP**

To loosen tough sod, hold the handle of a spade close to the ground and kick the blade. This will break up the soil more easily.

## TAMPER

A tamper has a square head with a long handle sticking up from its center. The tamper flattens and smoothes the ground as it presses down on loose soil.

## ROUND-POINT SHOVEL

This large shovel has a pointed steel head and is used for removing and depositing large amounts of soil or rock.

## WHEELBARROW

A wheelbarrow is very handy for moving and depositing soil, fertilizer, or even other tools. With two handles for pushing and a single wheel, the wheelbarrow makes it easy to carry heavy loads.

## GARDEN HOSE

You may think a garden hose is only used to spray water on a garden. A hose can also be helpful when marking a garden's edges. Simply lay your garden hose in the desired pattern on the grass and use your powdered chalk to trace it. Then follow the steps for lifting and removing the sod.

# OUTDOOR BUILDING

A backyard playhouse is the perfect place for outdoor fun. Measuring and cutting wooden beams are the first steps for this project. A tape measure, sawhorse, and handsaw take care of the job. A hammer and nails are used to put the beams together. A level checks that the frame is straight. A framing square helps make sure the wood panels for the walls and roof are measured correctly. After the wood panels are cut and nailed to the beams, a caulking gun fills in any gaps between the wood.

## SAWHORSE

A sawhorse is a sturdy steel or wooden frame that supports a piece of wood for cutting. Using two sawhorses provides better control and accuracy for the cut.

## SAWS

Saws come in many shapes and sizes. Using a pushing and pulling action, a person can use a saw to cut through a piece of wood or other material.

## HACKSAW

A hacksaw is shaped roughly like a rectangle. The thin blade of this tool is specially hardened to cut through metal or plastic pipes.

## HANDSAW

A handsaw has a sturdy wooden or fiberglass handle and a long, steel blade. The blade is edged with tiny, sharp teeth.

## COMPASS SAW

A compass saw has a pointed end that's perfect for cutting into the middle of softer material, such as the plaster on a wall.

## COPING SAW

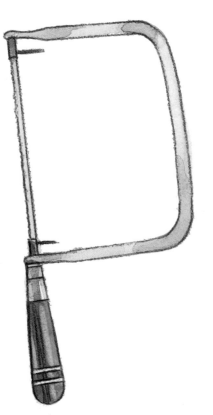

A coping saw is shaped like the letter P. It has a very thin blade that allows it to finely trim wood, creating curved or detailed designs.

# LEVEL

A level shows whether a piece of wood or other material is perfectly horizontal or vertical. Liquid is contained inside each section of the level. When the level is placed on a flat surface, a bubble in each liquid section begins to move. To indicate the surface is perfectly horizontal, the bubble should fall in the center of each section.

# PLUMB BOB

A plumb bob has a pointed weight attached to a long piece of string. It is used to check if a wall is perfectly vertical. The string is held at the top of the wall with the weight hanging down. Together, the string and the weight should form a perfectly straight line.

## TOOL TIP

Wood can also be held to a sawhorse with a tool called a vice. This is a metal clamp that can be adjusted to fit on thick or thin surfaces. Using a vice on a sawhorse leaves a person free to use both hands for cutting.

# FRAMING SQUARE

A framing square is used to measure a perfect square corner on one or more pieces of wood. Shaped like a giant letter L, this measuring tool can show whether or not two pieces of wood are joined correctly.

## COMBINATION SQUARE

A combination square is a measuring tool. It looks like a standard ruler with a sliding head attached. The head locks in place, letting you mark perfect angles and straight, even lines.

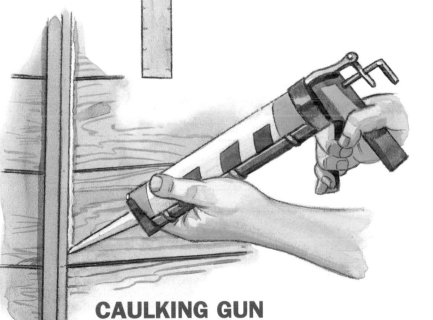

## CAULKING GUN

Caulking is a sticky material that hardens when it dries. It is used to seal an area against water and wind. Caulking is usually sold in a tube. The tube is placed inside a caulking gun, which squirts out the caulking when the trigger is squeezed.

# TOOL GLOSSARY

**adjustable wrench** • a hand tool with one fixed jaw and one moveable jaw; used to tighten or loosen nuts and bolts of different sizes (also called a "crescent" wrench)

**Allen® wrench** • an L-shaped steel bar used to tighten bolts and screws of various shapes and sizes

**ball-peen hammer** • a hand tool with a flat, steel face for pounding nails and a rounded steel face for bending and shaping metal

**bricklayer's hammer** • a type of hammer with a flat, steel end on one side of its head, and a sharp edge on the other; used to cut bricks and trim stones

**broadknife** • a wallpaper removal tool; also used to hold wallpaper in place when cutting a straight edge with a razor knife

**caulking** • a sticky material that hardens when it dries; used to seal an area against water and wind

**caulking gun** • a caulking dispenser that holds a tube of caulking and pushes out the product with the squeeze of a trigger

**chainsaw** • a power saw used to cut tree limbs or logs

**chalk line** • a string coiled inside a metal container filled with powdered chalk; used to mark a straight line on a surface

**circular saw** • a power saw with a spinning, disk-shaped blade; used for cutting wood and other materials

**combination square** • a measuring tool with an attached, sliding head; used to mark perfect angles and straight lines

**compass saw** • a handsaw with a pointed end; used for cutting into the middle of softer material, such as the plaster on a wall

**coping saw** • a handsaw with a very thin blade; used to finely trim wood and to create detailed designs

**dust mask** • a protective paper mask that fits over the nose and mouth and filters out dust and dangerous materials

**framing square** • a measuring tool used to mark a perfect, square corner on one or more pieces of wood

**garden edger** • a gardening tool used to cut through soil and roots

**garden hose** • a long tube that is attached to a water supply and is used to spray water on a garden; also used with powdered chalk to mark a curved line

**hacksaw** • a handsaw with a very hard, thin blade; used for cutting through metal or plastic pipes

**handsaw** • a hand tool with a long, steel blade that is edged with tiny, sharp teeth; used to cut through wood or other materials

**hand trowel** • a small shovel used to remove and deposit small amounts of soil

**hard hat** • a padded hat made from shock-resistant materials; used to protect the head from injury while working

**hearing protectors** • plastic or foam plugs that are placed in the ears to block out loud sounds; also available as padded earmuffs

**hoe** • a gardening tool used for chopping and weeding

**jigsaw** • a power saw with a thin blade that is used for making detailed, curved cuts in wood or other materials

**kneepads** • protective pads that provide a foam cushion to support the knees from pressure while working

**level** • a measuring tool that shows whether a surface is perfectly horizontal or perfectly vertical

**level head rake** • a gardening tool with steel teeth that is used to spread or break up soil, level garden beds, and remove debris

**linesman's pliers** • a hand tool used for gripping objects and cutting wire or metal

**mallet** • a type of hammer with a barrel-shaped head that is made of hard rubber, plastic, or wood; used to strike the end of another tool, such as a wood chisel

**mason's line** • a long, thin string made of cotton or nylon; used with powdered chalk to mark a straight line on a surface

**nail hammer** • a hand tool with a rounded steel end for pounding nails and a claw to remove them

**needle-nose pliers** • a hand tool with long, thin jaws that are used for holding and cutting; especially useful when working in tight spaces

**paint roller** • a metal tool with a foam, polyester, or wool cover; used to spread paint evenly across large areas

**paintbrush** • a painting tool with straight or angled bristles; used to apply paint on surfaces

**Phillips® screwdriver** • a hand tool that is specially made to fit into a screw with a small X on its head; used for driving a screw into or removing it from a hole

**pipe wrench** • a large, heavy hand tool with an adjustable jaw; used to grip and turn large bolts and pipes

**plane** • a trimming tool with a wide, sharp blade that shaves and smoothes a piece of wood

**plastic smoother** • a flexible plastic tool used for smoothing out wallpaper

**plumb bob** • a measuring tool that shows whether a surface is perfectly vertical

**powdered chalk** • a material that is sprinkled over a mason's line to mark a straight line on a surface

**power drill** • an electric tool with a spinning metal tip called a bit; used to make holes in wood or other materials

**pry bar** • a steel tool with a bent head that is used to pull off wood that has been nailed in place

**putty knife** • a hand tool with a flat, flexible blade; used to evenly apply a wet plaster called spackle over holes or cracks in a wall

**ratchet nut driver** • a hand tool that is specially made to fit into a screw with a squared slot on its head; used for driving a screw into or removing it from a hole

**razor knife** • a sharp blade that is used for cutting and trimming wallpaper

**round-point shovel** • a gardening tool with a pointed steel head; used to remove or deposit large amounts of soil or rock

**safety goggles** • protective glasses that fit over the eyes and guard against dust and flying bits of material

**sanding block** • a block covered with sandpaper; used to smooth surfaces by rubbing away bumps, bubbles, and rough spots

**sawhorse** • a sturdy steel or wooden frame that supports a piece of wood for cutting

**seam roller** • a wallpapering tool with a hard, plastic head; used to press on strips of wallpaper where they meet to prevent the edges from peeling

**sledgehammer** • a very large hammer with a rectangular head; used to pound large nails or spikes into a surface and to break up rocks

**slip-joint pliers** • a hand tool with a hinge that allows the opening of the jaws to change from wide to narrow; used to grip small objects; most commonly used pliers

**slotted screwdriver** • a hand tool that is specially made to fit into a screw with a single slot across its head; used for driving a screw into or removing it from a hole

**smoothing brush** • a wallpapering tool with short, coarse bristles; used to flatten out wrinkles or air bubbles in wallpaper

**socket wrench** • a hand tool with a rounded hole on its end; used to turn nuts and bolts of different sizes

**sod lifter** • a gardening tool with a bent handle and rounded head; used to cut into and remove a layer of sod

**spade** • a large shovel used for cutting into soil and digging

**strap wrench** • a type of wrench that allows you to turn objects of odd sizes

**tamper** • a tool with a heavy, square surface made of metal or wood; used to flatten and smooth soil or gravel

**tape measure** • a measuring tool made up of a thin, steel ruler coiled inside a metal or plastic case

**toilet plunger** • a plumbing tool with a rubber suction cup that is used to clear clogged drains

**tool belt** • a belt worn around the waist to provide easy access to tools; some may support back muscles while working

**utility knife** • a sharp blade housed within a protective case; used for cutting soft materials

**wheelbarrow** • a small vehicle with a single wheel and two handles for pushing; used to move and deposit heavy loads such as soil, fertilizer, or gravel

**work gloves** • protective coverings for the hands; can be made of rubber, heavy canvas, or leather

ISBN 0-439-28857-6

Text written by Kimberly Weinberger.
Illustrations by Tom LaPadula.
Copyright © 2001 by Homer TLC, Inc. All rights reserved.
Home Depot, The Home Depot, and the Orange Square Logo
are registered trademarks of Homer TLC, Inc.
Published by Scholastic Inc.
SCHOLASTIC, CARTWHEEL BOOKS, and associated logos
are trademarks and/or registered trademarks of Scholastic Inc.

Library of Congress Cataloging-in-Publication Data

Weinberger, Kimberly.
    Home Depot, Big book of tools / by Kimberly Weinberger; illustrated by Tom LaPadula.
        p.   cm.
    ISBN 0-439-28857-6
    "Cartwheel Books."
    1. Tools — Juvenile literature. 2. Home Depot (Firm) — Juvenile literature.
    [1. Tools 2. Dwellings — Maintenance and repair.] I. Title: Big book of tools.
    II. LaPadula, Tom, ill. III. Home Depot (Firm) IV. Title.

TJ1195 .W45 2001
621.9—dc21                                                      00-054740
10 9 8 7 6 5 4 3 2 1                              01 02 03 04 05